# TO KNOW HIM IS TO LOVE HIM

Gloria Marcella Perry-Hewitt

ISBN 979-8-88832-352-6 (paperback)
ISBN 979-8-88832-353-3 (digital)



Christian Faith Publishing
832 Park Avenue
Meadville, PA 16335
www.christianfaithpublishing.com

Printed in the United States of America

This book is dedicated to my beloved Marlon Alanso Hewitt. You will always have a place in my heart. Marlon, you were a friend to everyone around you. You even made sure your friends had a job at the nuclear plant where you worked for five-plus years. I even remember when you bought a few homeless men a pair of shoes and socks because your heart was so pure. That very next day you told me you wanted to open up a homeless shelter because it hurts you to see men homeless. Your heart was so pure that anyone could ask you to do anything and without hesitation, you would do it, even if you weren't feeling good. Although you had your good days and bad days you made sure your mother looked good and dressed well. I'm smiling now thinking about what you said to me: "My mother should have the best and look the best." You took the time out to find someone who does natural hair and find a couple of stores that you think I would like to shop at. I still shop there to this day. I will never forget the day after my hair appointment and after we went shopping for some new clothes; you told me I should write a book, a book that will tell the world about your struggles and successes. It's because of you my handsome son that I, we, have a book now.

Although the Lord called you home on November 30, 2022, at the age of forty-seven, your spirit still remains with me throughout the words of our book. The day you left, the pain you endured, the sleepless nights we both had, and the hospital visits and the day we laid you to rest will forever be embedded in my mind and heart. Your daughter, your son, your brother, and your family and friends all love and miss you.

Thank you for encouraging me to write this book.

Mommy loves you so much. It hurts just to write the dedication. Just know your memory, your legacy, your spirit will forever have a place in my heart.

I love you, my sweet Marlon!

# CHAPTER 1

# The Beginning

Tonight, I am starting once again with my book. I pray that God will give me the time, energy, wisdom, and understanding to finish this book, which I would like to use to share my experience and testify of God's blessings in my life. I know he is real, *for sure.* I know his Word is true, surely pure, and perfect.

I walk a treacherous journey but a protected one. With his love and mercy, he is ever so faithful to me every time I fail. Faith takes authority over the power he gave me—to stand on his word and be strong in the power of *his* might. Sometimes I feel discouraged over things that are not going well in my life. But I would hear God saying, "Be of Good Courage, Be Not Afraid, Fear Not. I am with you always. I will never leave you nor forsake you" (Deuteronomy 31:6).

I remember where he brought you from. Sometimes we have to take a stroll down memory lane, where the Lord brought us from.

I had a happy childhood; my brothers and sisters were loving and kind. My parents were tough on us to be loving and kind to each other.

I learned to extend love and kindness wherever I go; there is always someone that needs love and kindness or a shoulder to cry on.

In the book of Psalms, David said, "Cry unto the Lord!" He heard me and delivered me out of all my troubles. I was eighteen years old when I cried unto the Lord for help. He let me know that "when I consider thy heavens, the work of thy fingers, the moon and the stars, which thou hast ordained; What is man, that thou art mindful of him? and the son of man, that thou visitest him? For thou hast made him a little lower than the angels, and hast crowned him with glory and honour" (Psalm 8:3–5).

I remember he annotated me to go and feed his sheep. The Spirit will give me the right word to impart into them whether it is a physical, financial, or spiritual problem that most of us face.

Jesus told Peter to feed his sheep if he loved him. Sometimes they wander away, but we must find them, search for them, and love them as Jesus told us to do.

Philippians 4:11 reminds us of our calling as ministers, teachers, pastors, and apostles. This is a great calling for every believer. Every believer should know their calling. Mine was devotion, and I commenced early in the morning. I was talking with the Lord about the problems my son and I were going through. He reminded me that he is the reward of those who diligently seek him. He is the restorer, and he is the light that shines in my life. That light will never go dim because *he* created that light; what he created lasts forever.

Today I will tell my story of a broken heart that has been restored.

Looking back at the person you spent many years with, you should never feel alone, discouraged, or afraid because you are on a road to recovery and restoration.

The Bible always gave us wonderful stories of people who were abused and accused of things they did not do. Joseph was beaten by his brothers; he was accused by his master's wife. Anna was restored after years of a broken heart. The passage 1 Samuel 2 helps us to understand another example of God's work. Hannah prayed; she could not have children. She asked God to give her a son. Hannah's husband, Elkanah, loved her very much. Peninnah, the second wife, had many daughters. I would suggest you read the full story in the Bible. Hannah conceived and bore children. Eli, the priest, blessed Hannah and Elkanah and named the child Samuel. He became a great profit and a faithful priest. Oh, give thanks unto the Lord, for he is good. His mercy endureth forever.

# CHAPTER 2

# His Scarface

He lay down his life for us.

When the burdens weigh heavily, when the way seems dark and temptation seems unbearable, Jesus said, "Cast your care upon me because I care for you. They that wait upon the Lord shall renew their strength. They shall mount up with wings as eagles. They shall run and not be weary. They shall walk and not faint" (Isaiah 40:29–31). He is the rock when I run to the shelter; I am safe in the shelter of the storm.

I read Psalm 92:12–13, which caught my attention. It reads, "I must be righteous and shall flourish like a palm tree. He shall grow like a palm tree. He shall grow like the Cedar of Lebanon. Those that are planted in the house of the Lord shall flourish in the courts of our God." God created the palm tree stronger than any other tree to withstand any storm that comes its way. After the storm, the tree will straighten up and be stronger after the wind and rain. I have my Lord to help me through the storm and will help me to stand after the storm. Although it's not a pleasant situation to be in, he will see me through it all.

There are seasons for everything—seasons for snowstorms, hailstorms, and rainstorms. Most of these storms we know they are coming. I will prepare for them, but there came a storm, a personal storm—you know, the one I live and cannot prepare for. The storms may come up on us while we are unaware of them. But since I am a child of the Most High God, he watches over me and gives me his word. God said, "We must put on the whole armor of God. That we may be able to withstand against the wiles of this devil." Those words make me feel safe, strong, and confident that the storm will pass by me, leaving me unbroken.

The most important decision I made was when everything around me seemed hopeless. It was the time I had to put all my trust in God and believe that he would see me through. His word in Psalm 50:4 says that God is the same yesterday, today, and forevermore. He told great leaders and prophets that they will have troubles and trials to be of good courage.

# CHAPTER 3

# The Love of God

The Word of God reminds me that he is a God at hand and not a God of the far off. Just call on him, and he will be there. He is a great and loving God. I can truly say that he is the love of my life. No one can take that love from me. I hold on to his love daily. I am blessed to be a child of the Most High God, who is my healer, deliverer, and sustainer. His love keeps me safe and blessed; I have full assurance in him.

In 1992, I had a brain tumor that was life-threatening. If I did not take care of it early, it would have been fatal. For most people and me, it was frightening because it centered around all the major nerves. At the time that I learned about it, I had my husband and two teenage sons. The first thing I did after I received my prognosis was call on Jesus—my healer who heals all diseases.

I remember I was going to Bible school at the time. I told my professor what I learned about my tumor. He gathered the students to pray for me. He said, "Your daughter has a problem, and whatever way you see fit to dissolve it, we are going to trust you."

On my way from school, on the train, the Holy Spirit spoke to me and led me to read Proverbs 3:5–6. I felt better in my spirit knowing that I heard from God. I went to my doctor for a consultation, and after some test, both neurologists agreed that surgery would be needed—the sooner, the better. I asked God to give me the best possible surgeon to take the tumor out. My surgeon told me while looking at it that it was between an area surrounded by major nerves. He gave me a 50 percent chance of it coming out.

It was already causing noticeable problems with my vision and my balance. At that time, the Lord laid it on my heart not to share the information with everyone—only close family, my husband and two children and my sister, who were going to Bible school with me. I continued to seek the Lord as I prepared for surgery. I knew the Lord would shine his light on my path once I ask him for guidance.

My biggest fear was an unsuccessful surgery, and I remember his promise that he would provide me with courage and strength when I needed it the most. He promised me courage and strength when I needed them. Many nights I would be up pacing back and forth with wandering thoughts. Even though I knew better and the Lord had given me his assurance, I was still a mother that had concerns about leaving my two children behind. I purposed in my heart I'm going to trust him with all my heart. He is my rock, my shield, and my comforter. He gives me strength in times of weakness.

# CHAPTER 4

# Grateful

During the months of recuperation at home from surgery, every day I thanked God for being alive and told him how grateful I was and how I wanted my life to be a blessing to others. I remember a few years back, he gave me the scripture of Isaiah 41 and 43. It took me a long time to know what he was saying to me. Isaiah 41:15 got ahold of me, saying, "I will make you a new sharp thrusting instrument having teeth: Thou shalt thresh the mountains, and beat them small, and shalt make the hills as chaff."

After, I read Isaiah 43:10, "Seeing you are my witness says the Lord and my servant whom I've chosen that you may know and believe me and understand that I am he before me there was no God formed, neither shall there be after me."

He gave me Genesis 12, which told how Abraham left his kinfolk so God could use him for his purpose. I had no idea I was leaving to live in Florida. I came down to visit my sister. While visiting her, we were looking around to see some of the most beautiful houses in Central Florida. I was very much impressed with the different areas we visited. I told my husband I would love to live in Florida. It would also be better for my health because the cold and snow were becoming a health issue for me. We decided to move to Florida after much praying.

My nephew was living there when we made numerous trips back and forth to Florida. My nephew was of much help to us. He showed us a variety of communities. We stumbled upon a community where we decided to live. Even before moving to Florida, the Lord showed me visions of streets with houses that look like shacks on dirt roads and small broken-down houses.

In one of my visions, I saw an old lady sitting on a porch in a small broken-down house with a zinc roof as if she were waiting for someone. Thinking back to the scripture and vision the Lord gave me, I felt like he was preparing me for a mission. The place I saw in my vision resembled the place in Jamaica where I grew up.

I remember saying to the Lord, "Oh, Jamaica, I cannot drive there. I can't manage these hills and curves." I never shared this vision with anyone. But *God!* He showed me what he was about to do in my life. One day on my way to work, the Lord said, "Your work at New York University Medical Center is finished."

I repeated what I heard the Holy Spirit said as I walked down the street. The job that I loved, where I met people from all walks of life, was an opportunity for me to share the good news of salvation with everyone I encountered.

One day a coworker, who was the union delegate, said, "I don't have to work if I can't perform my job properly. I have enough years invested that I can do out on disability."

I never paid any attention to what he was saying until I decided to act on what he was telling me. I said, "Okay, I will see my doctor."

My union delegate made it clear to me that if I can't manage to work, I should let him know. I worked as long as possible with lighter duties. However, my equilibrium kept me off balance. One day on my way home from work, I lost my balance while waiting for the train to arrive. This was one of the scariest moments of my life. I lost my balance and almost fell on the train tracks. But *God!* Thank God for his protecting angels.

At that very moment, I decided to retire. I thank God for the favor he has given me throughout the transaction of my resignation. I also gave many thanks to those who were involved. Having brain surgery like mine was very expensive; however, much of it was paid through my insurance and benefits from my employer. I had to pay the rest out of my pocket to my doctor. He gave me a financial plan that I paid for a long time.

I thought about the bills that I needed to pay when I got to Florida. But God! He is the master planner and provider. He must be trusted in whatever we do, so let him be the center of our decision-making. He knows how to delete and cancel debts. I got a letter from my doctor saying, *"All debts are canceled!"* Nobody *but God! Only God* would do such miraculous works.

# CHAPTER 5

# Salvation

Heavenly Father, great Creator, how can I say thanks for the things you have done? You have given me so much, and your gifts of giving keep coming. You are so wonderful to me. I'm thankful for all your blessings. I thank you for entering my life in 1967, when you saved me and sealed me with your love.

I will never forget that afternoon when I was lying sick in my bed. You showed me Psalm 6, which was posted on a blackboard. I read verses 4 and 5, and it took ahold of me. It read, "Return to Lord, deliver my soul, oh save me for mercy's sake, for in death there is no remembrance of thee. In the grave who shall give thanks."

At that time, I was not feeling well. I might have been coming down with a virus. I was not a person who would normally read the Bible every day. A week later, I had a vision. I saw a hand stretched out to me near a pool of water. I looked up at a high mountain. I was compelled to make my way to the top of this mountain. As I looked up at this steep, slippery, and muddy mountain, it seemed impossible to reach my destination. I felt discouraged and began to cry. A song came into my heart, and I began to sing, "Are you worried and lonely, and don't know what to do? Just call on the Lord Jesus and he will carry you through. What he has done for others, he can do for you." After that song, I felt a peace and noticed that the branches started to materialize, and I began to climb off the mountain. I thought about what I have seen in the vision, and it confirmed that God gave me a calling to serve him. Ever since then, my life has not been the same. I was led to a church where I was baptized and became active in the ministry. I believe that God has given us a road map to follow and put us on this journey that we should not detour but follow the instructions.

Reading 2 Timothy 3:16 and 17, I realized that sometimes we try to put our lives together without reading directions; emotions and feelings cannot be trusted to lead us in the right direction. *I thank you, Lord,* for providing a clear set of directions for our lives. I am thankful for being able to read your Word, which provides the proper principles and understanding that make us creative and function correctly. I know that there is joy in the journey. I love to tell people about my visitation with the Lord. Years later, I finally understood the vision of the mountain. It was teaching me patience, assurance, faith, and courage.

In my life, I have encountered not only mountains but valleys, rivers, and storms that are very difficult to pass through. But the all-knowing God promises he will be with me through everything just as he did with David, Paul, the three Hebrew boys, and Daniel. He promised to form a wall of protection around us. There's nothing too hard that God cannot do. We must trust him completely with all our troubles and trials. He said in his words that we must take all our burdens to him.

One day when I was working in my garden, I suddenly became depressed because of how my marriage was going, not knowing at that time that my husband was going through medical problems that I was unaware of. The Spirit spoke to me and said, "In your cloudy day, there will be sunshine."

# CHAPTER 6

# Florida

After waiting for my house to be completed in Florida, it was exciting to have a house built from the ground up and ready to move in. After weeks of unpacking, I felt good about everything and gave God thanks. While leaving New York, everyone was wishing that I would relax and enjoy my new home. I assured them I was just not going to sit in my big beautiful white house and enjoy it because I knew God had work for me to do.

I remember on January 2, 1999, I did not know what or where to start. I was led by the Spirit to take some tracts and some Bibles to the south side of where I live. I drove slowly and stopped where people were hanging out in front of the store. I got out of my car and introduced myself. I let them know that I was new in town and would like to know more about the area. I had my tracts and Bible in the car. I offered them some tracts, and they took them. I told them that I was a minister and asked them if I could pray for them.

They were delighted with the offer and said, "Yes!" I prayed for them, and they thanked me and told me no one ever took the time to come around and pray for them, not even the local pastors. I felt blessed that God used me to encourage someone and showed me where to start. The next day, I went to another block and saw some others that needed help. I offered to help them, and they were grateful that I bought them food and clothes.

Weeks and months went by, I continued to meet interesting people, and I learned about their needs. Many of them couldn't read and were unemployed. Every time I drove past the oak tree, the same group of young guys were hanging out. Every time I stopped to talk to them, they would ask me for a prayer. These guys were young and were from different walks of life. Some of them were hustlers, and others were convicted felons. They all were reaching out for something that would better their life, all while reaching and searching for someone that cared. They were always thankful for me praying for them and spending time with them. Without hesitation, I would pray and ask God that he would save them and find them jobs. I can truly say that they were very respectable young men.

One day I decided to go to a street I haven't been to before. It was such a big complex that I decided to turn on the street not very far from the main road. As I drove slowly, I looked, and behold, there was a house I saw in my vision with a zinc roof and an old lady sitting on the porch. I stopped and went up to her with a look of disbelief. I introduced myself. We started to have a good conversation about the goodness of the Lord. I could not bring myself to let her know that God showed me her in my vision. To God be the glory for the things he has shown me.

Whether I was at the supermarket or the nursery, I would pray daily for them so that God would save them and find them jobs. No matter where I was, there would be someone who would recognize me and come up to me and hug me. They would remind me that I prayed for them under the oak tree. Some of them would say they are working, saved, or in a better situation. It was so many of them, but only a few had a place in my heart. I particularly remember there was a young lady around eighteen years of age. I remember seeing her sitting on the sidewalk on the side of the store crying and wearing dirty clothes. I asked her, "What's the matter?" She told me that she got beat up by one of the men that she dealt with, and they were making fun of her and humiliating her. I told her to get up, and while I held her in my arms, she wept on my shoulders.

She told me how she got herself into this predicament. I told her she would be all right. I went home and brought her some clothes and told her how we're doing this for Jesus and how he can deliver her out of this situation. A few days later when I was passing out tracts and Bibles, I saw the young lady again, and she asked me to give her a Bible. At that time, I did not have any more Bibles to give out. I knew I had to order more Bibles, but they would take a few weeks to arrive. During that time, I started to think about my personal Bible, which was a going-away present from my New York family, that I kept on my nightstand. This Bible was very pretty; it was white and had gold lettering on the cover. I went home and decided to bring her that Bible. She hugged me, and I told her to make sure she'd read it.

# CHAPTER 7

# The Word

What's even more exciting about the things I enjoyed was that I was able to share my story with friends in New York. My stories were so enlightening that they inspired my friends to move to Florida. I remember hearing stories of how they would pray and trust God for the day to move to the beautiful sunshine state in their new homes. It was my delight to be of service during their transition to Florida. Soon after their transition, I introduced them to a retiree club—Doris Turner retiree 1199 club—in Casselberry, Florida. In addition to their involvement with the club, we assisted them in finding a church of worship as well as in giving them some good Southern hospitality. The club also provided them medical supplies, such as blood pressure machines, diabetic kits, and many other health-care needs.

In fact, I remember my mother being an entertainer for the community. She got an inspiration on my willingness to be of service to my club and community. For some reason, I remember, during the summertime, she played folk dance, organized church activities, baked cakes, and made delicious chocolate and coconut candies. She was a happy and dedicated woman who accomplished a lot before she passed away. I most definitely felt the need to continue with her passion.

Since I am a retiree myself, I got more involved with the Christian community. In fact, I got even more involved with my club and became the vice president in 2021 and have helped over six other families to move to Florida from New York. I'm also a part of the planning committee that plans shopping trips; trips to the beach or to the museum; cruises; and many more activities for them to enjoy. It brought me great joy to see each family finally at peace and comfortable in the new environment. I love being of service to anyone in need or searching for assistance.

# CHAPTER 8

# Restore

Restoration came for me after years of unpleasant accusations from my unfaithful husband. I am now surrounded by happy and caring Christian people. After reading 1 Corinthians 2:5—"Your faith should not stand in the wisdom of men, but in the power of God"—I felt weakness, fear, and a lot of trembling. However, I had doubt that God is a restorer. As I look back on my journey of life, it was my memories that helped me through in good times and bad. It was only then that I turned to the Bible and studied God's Word every day. His words felt like medicine to my soul. It provided me a cure for the heartache and my weak mind and the power to help me through my difficult storms. After studying his Word, I've decided in my heart that I will never quit. I will ride out any storm that I encounter.

> Know ye not that ye are the temple of God and
> the Spirit dwelt in you. (1 Corinthians 3:16)

I'm absolutely sure that when someone loves you, they never give up on you. Without a doubt, I know God loves me, and he will never give up on me. For the past twelve years, I have been the sole caregiver of my husband, who suffered from dementia. I find it very hard to describe the twelve years; I didn't know how much time was left for him. It is a journey I will never forget, and I would not recommend it to anyone.

It's a hard test of the soul, spirit, and mind to watch a loved one go through this long-suffering illness. You must have all the faith that you can muster and true dedication to the person whom you live for. I can only give God thanks for his love and mercy, for giving me wisdom and understanding, and for his care. In my weakness, he gave me strength. In my fear, he gave me hope. In my doubt, he gave me faith to trust him. In Psalm 31:24, it states, "In the middle of the night when there are no saints around, thy shall pray with me."

God told me to be of good courage: "Fear not, be not afraid. I will be with you always." During those years of caring for my husband, I learned to depend on God for everything. I know for sure that he keeps my mind steadfast in him. When I needed help with my husband and did not get any assistance, I can recall Psalm 121 saying, "My help cometh from the Lord, which made heaven and earth keep Israel shall neither slumber nor sleep." I am glad that I can call on him anytime and anywhere because he said, "When you call, I will answer." I remember a late night when my husband was restless and could not sleep, I tried to call upon the Lord for help. He heard my cry, and my husband went to sleep. If I go through the fire, I will not be burned. When I go to the water, it will not overflow me. I've been through many storms in my days, *but God* always comes to my rescue. He is my lifeboat; if I'm drowning in my physical, spiritual, and financial troubles, he delivers me. That comes from being fortunate enough to know him, and truly knowing him is to love him. To be honest, sometimes I'm looking for instant deliverance and do not know how it works. I know that the Most High God lives within my heart and that whatever comes my way, I am more than a conqueror, a victor, and not a victim. Philippians 4:19 says that God shall supply all my needs according to his riches and glory through Christ Jesus.

I believe with all my heart. I have experienced the worst financial problems for a long time. I needed to trust him because his word is true. As soon as I thought a bill was paid off, there comes another unexpected bill. For example, my air conditioner broke down down, my roof fell in, and my waterline bust. I can go on and on and on with a list of my problems. Although I was stressed and worried, I could still hear the Lord say to me of good courage, "I have called you and ordained you. You will never walk alone. I am with you always." I know that I've been through many stones in my life, *but God* is with me. He told me he would bring me out to a wealthy place. I thank him for his unlimited grace and mercy because he looked beyond my fault and saw my needs.

To know him is to love him!

# CHAPTER 9

# Healing

I remember after my husband passed away, it was a very difficult time for me. During my bereavement, I felt lonely, and I needed my husband to put his arms around me like our first years of marriage. Those were the good times we shared. I felt like I was wrapped in a warm blanket, secure and safe. According to 1 Corinthians 3:9,

> For we are labourers together with God; ye are
> God's husbandry, ye are God building.

I see myself as God's building, and I will build with the best materials there is: faith and belief.

> Know ye not that you are the temple of God and
> the Spirit of God dwelleth in him. (1 Corinthians
> 3:16)

There were no more caress or romantic whisper in my ear to say, "You are my little mud flower" or "Mrs. Hewitt, how you are a blessing from above." Then I realized that is his caresses and whispers of romance in my ear were temporary.

The Word of God reminds me that His love is everlasting. No one can love me like Jesus, who gave His life for me. In those moments of sadness and loneliness, my God let me feel his presence all around me. I made a vow to God and man that I would keep away from the things that would defile my body: adult fornication and other things that served me no good.

After forty-two years of marriage, I was exhausted from being a longtime caregiver. I needed more than ever to have some alone time with God. I wanted to find a quiet place, where I would be able to heal and hear God's guidance. So I decided to go on a ten-day retreat in Silver Springs, Florida. I told my family where I was going; they could not call, and I was not able to use my phone or watch television. My time there would be fully in the presence of God. This retreat would be a time to remember.

My room was on the last floor of the building, overseeing the lake with a beautiful sky view. I remember praying to God for what he was about to pour into my spirit. The chapel at the retreat was open, and many times, I was there alone praying. Surprisingly, while praying, I started to feel the presence of the Lord during my walks in the woods along the orange trail to sit in the gazebo to see the streams of clear water running down its sides. That was one of my favorite places to pray while I was there communicating with God on a higher frequency. It was at that moment when things started to become clearer.

The voice said,

> What shall I cry for. There for is like the flower of the fields. The grass withered, the flowers fadedth because the spirit of the Lord blowers the opponent. Surely the people is grass. The word of God shall stand forever. Lift up your eyes on high and behold who has created the things. A number that brings out their host by numbers. You call all names by the greatness of His might. For that he is strong in power, not on faileth but they wait upon the Lord renewing their strength. They shall mount up with wings as eagles. They shall run and not be weary. They shall walk and not faint. (Isaiah 43:2)

When I left, I felt stronger and more confident in my mission.

One of my favorite scriptures is Psalm 34:8, "Oh taste and see that the Lord is good." I say this all the time because it is true in my life. I have experienced his goodness through his mercy and his healing. I have also seen how good he is through his blessings and consistent deliverance in times of trouble. There are "no boundaries in God's love." When I was facing difficulties and it was hard for me to relate to close family members, I could only look to God, who knows my innermost being. He knows me since I was in my mother's womb. He knows the path that is meant for me to take.

I remember seeing his hand stretched out to me, pulling me into his marvelous light. When his light shined on me, it reminded me that even if it doesn't shine as bright on the outside, it still shines in my soul. In fact, one night, I was looking up at the sky and saw his beautiful stars in the sky. I started to look forward to seeing them every night during my time at the retreat. However, it was one particular night I looked up at the same sky, and there were no stars. God was showing me something that even though the stars were not visible, they were still present. That taught me a valuable lesson—that he is still God at all times. At times I feel like I'm going through a dark tunnel, but his light will shine on me.

I love the Lord. He has heard me and answered my prayers. As a result from my time at the retreat, I gained a stronger love for the Lord, and I knew from this point forward that he would hear me and answer my prayers.

One particular situation week after the retreat, I found out that my son was having heart problems. As I mentioned before, I knew that my God is a healer because he is a specialist of the body he created. He is the healer of all wounds. I am for certain that we already have the blessings of the Lord. He told us in Psalm 1:12 that wealth and riches shall be in the house and his righteousness endure forever. When we read and study the Word of God, we get the understanding that God loves and blesses all of us. His children always know that God is our prover. He provides healing and protection. He gives us peace and joy and all the wonderful plans he has for our life. I'm personally committed and delighted by his promises to me. He says,

"He will not withhold any good thing from us." While walking with God, remember the most important thing: to seek him with all our heart, and we will find him.

I can remember when I looked back on the wonderful things that he has done for me and my family. I was going through some heavy burdens, but he promised to lift my burdens, and he will turn my mourning into dancing and my weeping into joy. He promised to bring it to past. His words are my strength, and there is power in the name of *Jesus*. Even if you call his name ten times, Jesus is there. His name has power, life, deliverance, healing, mercy, and victory all in his name. There is no greater love than Jesus's love.

# CHAPTER 10

# When He Speaks

I have experienced how he has turned my troubles into victory.

He said that the righteous shall flourish like a palm tree. I can hear him saying, "Fear not, be still and know that I am God." I felt his presence like he was beside me. When God speaks to you in whatever way or wherever you are, it will never be the same. With your confidence, your faith, and your weakness, my insurance will grow brighter every day. Cry out for help, and he will fight your battle. He never denies your call. He said the battle is not yours but his to fight.

I remember a few years ago when I left my home in Florida to go to New York to celebrate my sister's birthday. In the midst of the celebration, I suffered an aneurysm. *But God* was present to help. It was a very unhappy time for the family while celebrating one of my sister's birthdays. The Bible says that he will present help in times of trouble. At the party, there was a huge place where people celebrated all different kinds of functions. This particular building was equipped with an ambulance outside and inside that had oxygen. They even had nurses and ministers available.

I did not lose consciousness. I was taken in the ambulance accompanied by my brother to the hospital. At the hospital, I went through a CAT scan, and I was immediately put into an induced coma. I knew that my life was in God's hands. I was transferred to another hospital. The best brain surgeons were available. However, a surgeon specialist was not available to do the procedure, so one had to be flown in. When he arrived, he took a look at it and immediately went to my family. He told them that it doesn't look good. There's only a 5 percent chance of me surviving. But my family, who always prays, asked God to anoint the surgeon during the procedure. He looked at them and said, "I am anointed." At the moment, my family gave him permission to do the surgery. They never gave up; they were praying and waiting. After six hours, he came out and told them that I am going to be all right. They were giving God praise and glory.

After three days, I woke up. And I saw my family around me with smiles on their faces. Later on, when I woke up again, I saw my two sons, who were both in Florida. This was the one thing that really surprised me and touched my heart; my son, who has a childhood fear of flying, was right by my side. He did something that he said he would never do to be by his mother's side.

When I woke up again, they did not tell me the severity of the operation they just went through. They finally told me a few days later. They actually took their time to explain to me how the operation went. After explaining that everything was going to be all right, he informed my family that he would have to do another surgery. This second surgery would be a minor one. He wanted to make sure he had cleared everything out and to recheck his work.

# CHAPTER 11

# Perfect Love

God's perfect love binds us until eternity. What a perfect love I have! I will always cherish his love. I thank God for his blessings, the seen and unseen, and for the courage, faith, and belief. When things are at the lowest point, you should cast all your cares upon him.

During my recuperation, I experienced love and mercy of like I've never felt before. I was in my glory to know that I was so loved. Everyone from the doctors, nurses, everyone in the medical staff, and even my family (from my sisters, nieces, nephews, and cousins) were at my side night and day. Never, at one moment, was I alone. It brought me comfort and joy to always see both of my sons at my bedside. It was as if the presence of God was covering me at every moment.

Jesus is the author and finisher of my faith. I remember when the Holy Spirit would spoke to my heart on this one occasion, I heard him say, "Where I send my word, it would not return unto me void. The word of God is true." There is power in his word. The Lord touched my spirit while I was lying in my bed after a morning devotion. He showed me a ship in the Mediterranean Sea. The Lord told me to pray for the safety of the crew and the ship. I did as I was instructed to do.

It was a few weeks later that I learned that there were pirates in the area that were hijacking ships that were delivering imported cargo to different areas in the region. This ship was delivering food and other needed supplies, such as medical supplies to the poor in the area. A couple of days later, I learned the ship was rescued by another ship that was in the area. Thank God for the great things he has done and can do. To know God is to love him. My love for God is more than words can utter. God said in his Word that whenever he sends his word, it would not return void. It is so true.

The Bible shows on many occasions with individuals, townland wars, and prophets that God is our source and the master of everything. He is the planner and the great designer. My life was planned before I was born. Thank God for his mercy and love. Looking back on the journey in my life, God was always there for me when I fell. He picked me up and gave me strength. He is my potter; he never stopped molding me. We are not perfect, so we need him for our journey through life. The great men of God's prophets and leaders' assignments were not easy, but with faith in God, it was accomplished—men such as Abraham, Moses, David, and the son of God, Jesus. David's journey was not easy, but God was with him along his journey.

There were times in my life when I saw my children experience health problems. I would cry out unto God, who is the healer. I knew he heard my cries because he said before, "He told us to come to him and he will restore our thy needs." I prayed to him to restore my kids' health. I knew he was full of mercy and compassion. Many times I asked the Lord to search for and show me my weakness so that I can be stronger and more effective in my ministry.

As I study the Word of God and how it applies to my life, I experienced a deeper abiding love and joy than ever before. As a songwriter says, "Faith is the victory that overcomes the world." I can truly say that in my life, faith is my victory. I have overcome troubles, trials, heartache, and pain. Because of my faith in God, I'm writing this book to share my victories and blessings. I give God praise and glory for all the days of my life.

Psalm 1:3 says that "he shall be like a tree planted by the rivers of water that bringeth forth fruit in his seasons. His leaf shall not wither, and whatsoever do it, it shall prosper."

Jesus is the author and finisher of my faith. To know God is to love him. My love for God is more than words can utter. God said in his Word that whenever he sends his word, it would not return void (Isaiah 55:11). This statement holds true to whomever believes God's deliverance.

# CHAPTER 12

# Deliverance

I remember my first session of therapy after surgery like it was yesterday. They sent me home to complete the rest of the therapy as an outpatient. My sister allowed me to stay with her during this time. She was very kind and patient to allow me to live with her during my recovery period. She allowed me to stay downstairs, where it was peaceful and quiet. However, when my sister did her volunteer work, a few days out of the week, I really felt alone. I would sit and wonder why I didn't hear from any of my friends and why they didn't call to see how I was doing—the same friends for which I would go out of my way to help whenever they needed me. I would visit them in the hospital and pray for them. I would give them a ride to the supermarket, and none of them called to check on me.

I could remember the Lord saying, "I will repay you." I can also recall many years ago while living in Michigan, I would dream of my grandmother saying, "Let's pray." Every time I dream of her and her saying that, I would wake up the next morning on the floor in a praying position. So this one particular morning, I decided to write a letter to Jesus. I asked him to make me a loving, kind, forgiving, and understanding person to serve him until I see him in glory. All I remember was that I wrote this in red ink.

It wasn't until one day while in my bed complaining, the Lord said to me, "Do you remember the letter you wrote to me in red ink?"

I was in a state of shock and amazement. I said, "I can't believe you remember it." I was asking the Lord, who knows all things and sees all things. I laughed, and I cried, and I gave him thanks for loving and caring for me. I also told him I needed to go home to Florida, to my big house where I could walk around and dance and praise him. He reminded me about Peter, who was in prison in a cell, where he praised him and was delivered. I imagine Peter's cell was so small; he couldn't move around to dance. But through praying and worshiping *God*, his prison doors were open.

# CHAPTER 13

# The Power of Prayer

After the aneurysm, I had to go to rehab for therapy for a few days. During the time of therapy, I had some very excruciating pain. This pain was so bad that we would have to travel the expressway to get to where we were going. Some days were full of pain and loss of balance. However, during my recovery time, things were slowly restoring themselves.

On my annual visit to the doctor, he recommended the next date be our follow-up surgery. With the love and concern for me, he told me that this surgery wouldn't take long; they would just be removing the tissue. The Bible says that we should pray for one another. I called my church and asked my prayer ministry to pray for me while I'm preparing myself for the next day's surgery.

I found it necessary to go boldly before God and ask him to search my heart for anyone that I have not forgiven. I knew that my life was in his hands, and I was trusting him and his scripture to guide the surgeon's hands. Psalm 121:1–3 was my scripture at that time.

> I will lift up mine eyes unto the hills, from whence cometh my help. My help cometh from the Lord, which made heaven and earth. He will not suffer thy foot to be moved: he that keepeth thee will not slumber.

Since I believed in God's powerful words and the power of prayer, my surgery was a success. In fact, while waiting in the ICU, my surgeon told me that everything went well and all the tissues were removed. Also, if I wanted to go home, I could. Just hearing those words alone brought joy and happiness to my soul. Surprisingly, the ICU nurse told me that if I worked in that same position for a long time, it could only be God's favor. Goodness and mercy for sure are the things God had over me. At that moment, I knew for sure that God is a wonder-worker and he keeps his promises to be in the business of being a miracle worker.

Unquestionably, the good news had me so excited that I immediately called my family to come pick me up. They all were just as shocked and excited as I was, knowing I just got out of surgery a few hours before. In this case, I had to assure my family that the doctor said it was okay to go home. There was so much joy that filled my heart just knowing that my family was just as excited as I was. We all gave God the praise and glory for the great things he has done.

To know him is to love him!

# Testimony

It was January of 2013 that I would travel from Florida to Uptown, New York, to have my annual visit with my neurologist. Since this was after my two surgeries, I couldn't fly. My only form of transportation was either car or train; therefore, I decided to go by train.

Although I never knew where I would meet someone—on the train, at the streets, in the stores, or at a restaurant—I would always carry biblical tracts in to share. The Bible says that we should testify of him. Seeing that I am a child of God, he would always place people around me that are willing to hear his goodness. Throughout my traveling days, I have met quite a few interesting people that would call me to this day to ask me to pray for their marriage, business, health issues, and other problems. I didn't have a problem praying for whomever and whatever they ask for.

I particularly remember going to Laurelton, New York, to a West Indies restaurant, meeting a couple who just started their business. My server was the wife and owner of the establishment. As she began to take my order, she looked directly into my eyes and said, "You are a special person, and you have a smile and joy about you. God's light will always shine on you." In fact, I never told her who I was, and before I could say anything else, she introduced me to her husband. They both seemed to be happy running their own business. Just as she brought me my check, she asked me to pray for their business to prosper. Upon finishing my prayer, her face lit up, and she promised me she would stay in contact with me to let me know how her business was doing.

As a matter of fact, a year later, I went back to visit the same restaurant and saw that the business had expanded and they had hired more people to work with them. I knew that following God's instructions—to pray for others and share is his goodness—I would be a blessing to others. My God made me to complete his mission—to serve and feed his sheep. It brings me so much joy, happiness, and peace praying for individuals and sharing my testimony.

Meanwhile, still in Laurelton, New York, I went to in a cell phone place called Uconnect, and a gentleman came in and was admiring me and complimenting me on how I looked very nice. We got into a conversation about the goodness of God and understanding God's Word. The Bible tells us that wisdom is good, but with all our getting, get understanding. On my visitation home, I got more understanding of my life. It wasn't until during my visit to New York that I heard God telling me that I was one of his sheep that need to be fed. It was that very message I needed to hear that gave me the clarity. I needed to understand the purpose of my life.

He brought me forth also into a large place; he delivered me, because he delighted in me. (Psalm 18:19)

It was summer 2014 when I wanted to start traveling by plan. I had to consult this with my doctor. Since my sister had asked me during a really hot summer, I knew I didn't want to travel by car or train. I want to get to Jamaica as soon as possible. But since I was traveling to see my brother-in-law and celebrate his sixtieth birthday and the flight was only one hour, my doctor gave me permission to fly. I was very excited to get permission because I haven't been home in many years.

Nevertheless, my four sisters, a cousin, and I boarded the plane, and to my surprise, I had an entire row to myself. This moment, I started to feel alone and almost started to worry, but the Holy Spirit said to me, "Fear not, I am with you." Now, I started to pray for a safe flight. Immediately following my prayer, the Lord said, "If I didn't want you to come, I wouldn't let you."

Matthew 14 states that Jesus walked on water. When the people saw Jesus walking on the sea, they were troubled, saying "It is a spirit." They also said that Jesus spoke to them and said, "Fear not of good courage, it is I, be not afraid."

My sister came to see me and ask me if she could sit beside me. I said I was fine. The flight was very smooth and pleasant. On arrival, I felt a sense of joy in my spirit to be home. It is another expecting time with my family and friends whom I haven't seen for a long time now, especially my high school friends, if they ever came back home to visit their families.

# CHAPTER 15

# Retreat

One thing I'm very sure of is that God always loves his children the best.

There's a beautiful hotel called Grand Bahama hotel in Jamaica that's not too far from my birthplace—Kingston, Jamaica. I was there visiting for my brother-in-law's sixtieth birthday. This hotel was one of the largest and most beautiful hotels I'd ever seen. As a matter of fact, this hotel is known for people who travel from all over the world. On this one particular visit, my room was on the fifth floor overlooking the beach. What a beautiful view to wake up to every morning. As a matter of fact, I would take advantage of this view every morning and ask the Lord to lead me to someone that needs to hear his word for the day.

When I would talk to the Lord's chosen one, they would tell me they loved talking to me. It was at that moment I knew God can use me wherever I go. For this reason, I enjoyed sharing conversations with people I randomly met. And every time I did speak with someone, a special verse I used to hear in my mother's church would pop into my head, almost like a confirmation. The verse was, "People need people after a broken heart. People need people after a broken dream. People need the Lord." I smiled and praised God for allowing me to do his works.

I enjoyed my trips to and from the hotel and birthplace. It allowed me to see God's beautiful creation: river falls, fruits, hills, and mountains. God's Word is very true. He said weeping endureth for a night, but joy cometh in the morning (Psalm 30:5). I remember it was the morning after the death of my husband, after the visit from my trip, I was ready to return to Florida. We boarded the plane, and before takeoff, the pilot said, "There was a slight delay between three to five hours." However, we left about twenty-five minutes later. Within thirty to forty minutes of the flight, the pilot announced that there was a rainstorm in Orlando, and as soon as it cleared, we would land. I knew that the Lord took me out there and he would bring me back safely. I also knew that I was under the shadows of the almighty covariance; he gave his angels charge over us to keep us in all thy ways.

Once we landed safely and left the plane, there was a power outage, and we had to stay in customs for a while. We couldn't get our luggage because the belt in the terminal wasn't working. We were in customs for three to four hours. While waiting for the power to come back on, people were complaining that they would miss their connecting flight. And because of the long walk to the pickup area, my cousin and sister used a wheelchair. Considering we all didn't sit together on the plane, they didn't know I didn't eat or had anything to drink. Keep in mind that I am a diabetic. I became very thirsty, so I needed some water. I took my sister's walking cane and walked up to the desk. There was staff waiting for the power to come back on so we could get our luggage. I asked for a bottle of water, and they told me that they couldn't give the passengers anything.

By this time, I was getting weaker and just needed a bottle of water. I had to repeat myself, and that was when they decided that they could call the paramedics. I made it clear that I didn't need the paramedics, I just needed a bottle of water. The front desk still refused to listen. That was when I asked to speak with their supervisor. The clerk said she would get back to me. I waited for a while before the supervisor came to the front desk. I had to explain to them that there were diabetic people like myself and small children that needed water and something to snack on. The supervisor stated that no one was allowed to leave or come into customs and that goes for food as well.

As my conversation continued with them, I started to point out that if there was a great storm coming, would they allow all these people to perish because of their policy? A gentleman overheard my conversation and said he also was diabetic and would like some water. I went back to sit; a few minutes later, the attendant came back with another supervisor and said we would get the customs officer. They asked for my name, and a few minutes later, they bought a bottle of water.

During my wait, they explained that the airline did not carry water and they would have to borrow it from another airline. It was about fifteen to twenty minutes later, I heard them coming back saying they had water for all the passengers. Everyone started to shout, "Yes, water!" I looked around to see that the kids had nothing to eat on. So I told my niece to go to the attendant and ask for some cookies. To my surprise, she came back with cookies for all the kids. All the adults were jumping up for joy. After hours of waiting, everyone finally had cookies and water.

*But God!* Just as we were singing our praises, within a few minutes, the power was restored, our luggage began to come out, and people began to feel a sense of relief. I believe that God has an assignment for each one of us. All we have to do is to ask where and how he would like us to serve. Our gift should not be limited to those in Corinthians 12:8.

After the trip, I went home to thank God. I thought it was okay to go ahead and praise him on how he guarded us on the trip and how he used me in such a time like that. I will never forget Psalm 100:2, "All will serve the Lord with gladness."

# CHAPTER 16

# Final Results

The power of prayer has changed my life completely.

The Lord said that we must come to him and pray. I will never decline an opportunity to pray. The Lord said, "I have given you my word and everything that I have ever needed is in the word." While serving with passion, I have kept my eyes focused on him, not on the gifts but what he has given me: the ability to help others understand what he has shaped me into doing.

God created me for good works. Ephesians 2:10 helps me to understand that he prepared things for me in advance. He wanted me to complete several tasks in his kingdom. He gave me courage to take hold of those tasks. As I look back, I've learned that the Lord has revealed a few things to me and has kept me from places where I should not go.

One detailed moment that stands out was, after a few months of marriage, my husband was in a serious accident in Jamica while I was living in America. As newlyweds, I thought I should take time off from my job and be by my husband's side. When I talked to him, he insisted that I shouldn't come to be with him and that he would be okay. I was very perplexed at the thought of him saying such a thing. It was hard for me to understand why my husband wouldn't want me to be his side—I'm his wife. As I sat there thinking and trying to figure a way, the Lord made it where I couldn't go. It was a couple of years later, everything was revealed; there was another lady by his side the entire time, and he didn't want me to know. However, since I am a child of God and believe in my vows "till death do us part," I kept the faith. I was with him for forty-two years and had two handsome boys while having a victory in Jesus.

There was another unforgettable moment that I remembered. On my way to the doctor's office, I heard the Spirit say, "I have good news!" I was shocked to hear this, so I kept on going to the doctor's office. This was my last visit to see my surgeon, and I had to be there before 9:00 a.m. to do my lab work in the MRA. Since I was early, the test was completed before the doctor was scheduled to see me. While waiting in a room for more than an hour and half, I prayed to the Lord, asking him to let the doctor give me every two years to see him instead of one year. As soon as I finished and opened my eyes, my doctor came in with five students.

He looked at the MRA, instructing the students to look at it the first time before seeing the test. While they were looking, I asked the doctor if I could say something. He said, "Of course, you can. Go right ahead." I looked at the students and at my doctor. I said, "This doctor is the best. Learn from him. A few years ago, I had an aneurysm with 5.5 percent chance of survival. I am here now because of him. This doctor was created by God for this gift and purpose." They looked at me with amazement.

A moment later, the doctor said to the nurse practitioner, "What do you have today?" He looked at the chart and then at the monitor. He turned and said to me, "How old are you, Mrs. Hewitt?" I gracefully told him my age. Then, with a smile on his face, he said, "I don't see anything more to do or research." I had never seen anyone as happy as the doctor, five students, and nurse practitioner. I hugged everyone and praised God for his goodness. It was like having a church revival. My doctor said he couldn't have done it alone. We all were praising God for answering our prayers. He also said if you did come back, it should only be to give everyone a big hug and update on what I was doing.

# CHAPTER 17

# His Glory

As I look back at what I've been through and by many ordeals, I can truly say the plan that the Lord had for me is beyond my wildest dreams. He spoke blessings in my life and showed me things and places I would go. He promised to hold me with the right hand of his righteousness, and some things do not always work the way they should. Romans 8:38–39 said,

> For I am persuaded that neither does not live nor angels nor principalities no powers nor things to come nor deaths or any other creature shall be able to separate me from the love of God which is in Christ Jesus our Lord.

One of the most enlightening things I could remember is the Spirit giving me a word or a song that would show me what to expect from the visit to the doctor. The Holy Spirit would let me know all is well and let not my heart be troubled. Sometimes gospel songs and joy bells would ring my soul during my quiet time. It would instantly take me back to the many years God rescued me from great danger. Dangers or situations that only I could tell you the story of. The Bible said, "Goodness and mercy shall follow me all the days of my life" (Psalm 23:6). I can testify to that.

Evaluating the works and the times I put into my ministries, I promised the Lord I would honor my vow. There's always a reward, and there's always an award, so whatever you do for God, just know that he is watching. For example, wherever I go, there is always someone to remind me of the things I did for them and how much it was greatly appreciated. Sometimes I would receive thank-you cards and gifts for our ministry from people I had met on different occasions. Some of them would consist of gifts that I would donate to my ministry. No matter what it is, I made sure I tell God "thank you." While giving thanks to God, I could go to the store and find a close parking space or I could find an unexpected manager special or, even better, I remembered looking for something in my purse and a gentleman behind me said, "Ma'am, don't worry. I will pay for your groceries."

The Bible says, "Cast pasta bread upon the water, workout shall find it after many days" (Ecclesiastes 11:1). Romans 11:36 says that when we do all we can, the reason for everything comes from God alone. Everything lives by his power, and everything is for his glory.

I observed that most of the time people who knew me and knew what I've been through would go out their way to help me build a bigger and better ministry for God's glory.

Although I had a small church, the teaching ministry, I was happy to resume the Woman on a Mission ministry. The Lord spoke to me and told me to form a United Church Prayer coalition. This coalition would share the gospel with other believers, churches, our nations, and ministries around the world. Our activities included retreats, cruises, state parks, and other places where we would encourage people to join us in this great movement of God.

Our coalition would recruit our new members via the radio, email, mailed letters, phone calls, and handwritten cards. When we had our monthly meeting, our members would pray for our spiritual leaders, our nation leaders, our president, and other leaders around the world. We even had different believers from different churches join us as we prayed for churches and different necessities in the community. We would call leaders in other countries to pray with us so we all could be on one accord.

> Again I say unto you, That if two of you shall agree on earth as touching any thing that they shall ask, it shall be done for them of my Father which is in heaven. (Matthew 18:19)

# CHAPTER 18

# Faith of a Mustard Seed

Faith in God has always been a turning point in my life. He has made it clear that one should commit their all in whatever we are called to do and that we should always delight in it. When God gave us his words in Psalm 37:4, "Delight thyself in the Lord, and he will give you the desires of your heart," he means just that. Undeniably, when you have a faith of a muster seed, faith will be the victory that helps us overcome our troubles, heartache, and any pain that we might endure. However, with that faith, we should always remember that "faith without works is dead" (James 2:26).

In fact, because of my faith in God, I'm able to write this book and share my victories, miracles, and spiritual awakenings I have experienced throughout my life. I liked when God provides us with proven examples of having faith in the Bible. For instance, God shows us that Abraham was a man of faith. Abraham had enough faith that he was willing to sacrifice his only son. Because he had that much faith in God, he was able to provide a lasting sacrifice through his son—for Abraham and for all of us.

In addition to having the same faith of Abraham, I knew that one day he would call on me to do something or go somewhere; and when he did, I should be obedient. My obedience allows me to look back on my spiritual journey and see that I have overcome many obstacles. Despite those uncomfortable obstacles, I continue to read and study the Word of God. He has shown me on several occasions that there are rewards ahead if I am obedient. There were many times I've had conversations with Jesus, asking him how I can serve him in the best way possible.

He led me to becoming a believer in him. To be called a believer comes with great challenges throughout life. A great test was my vows before God and my husband. There were several times my husband and I considered to file for divorce. Since I believed in God and knew he would not leave me nor forsake me, we did not get a divorce, and I continued my love and trust in God. As believers of the high, Jesus will provide the tools we need, and he will also send us the Holy Spirit and power to stay strong in any trial. He will deliver miracles in your life, as he has done in mine. He will also make us into believers like he did David, who was anointed by God for a purpose.

Every day of my life, I thank God for my journey—whether the good or bad times, he has brought me through it all. He knows when we are weak, strong, sad, and impatient. Since he knows all, we should put our trust in him that he will stand on his promises. There shouldn't be any doubt in asking God to show us the vision for our future. We should always believe that God has something good waiting for us. All we need to do is open our arms and be ready to receive them. We should also, empty ourselves of disbelief and discouragement, all while knowing that God is ready and willing to bless our lives and to be a blessing to others.

There were many times the Lord called me to come to him and he blessed me. I was glad to be up that mountain. My song was, "Take all your troubles to Jesus and he will carry you through." I thank God for the power of active faith. The power of active faith in our life's journey should be bold of faith, which is already in *us*. Without faith, works are dead. I learned to go boldly before the throne of grace. It gives me inspiration as 1 John 5:4–5 says,

> For whatsoever is born of God overcomes the world and this is the victory that overcomes the world even our faith. But he that believeth that Jesus is the son of God.

I thank God for his remarkable Journey. I will always share the miracles and gifts I have experienced with others. I thank God for all the victories I have accomplished.

The author's name is Gloria Marcella Perry-Hewitt. She was born in Kingston, Jamaica, and completed Xavier High School in 1967. She continued her studies at Bronx Community College in New York. She also went to New York University, where she studied to be a dietary assistant.

Then she went to Hugee Theological Institute, where she received her bachelor's degree in theology. At the present, she is a prayer group minister in Apopka, Florida; the vice president for the retiree club; and an active member of Jamaican American Association of Central Florida.

If she could leave you with any Bible verse, it would be Matthew 18:19. He gives us a clear view of what we are going to do as believers. God will respond to our prayers. When the world is facing spiritual problems, health problems, and financial problems, only God will show us how much his love and compassion will deliver and restore his people.

* 9 7 9 8 8 8 8 3 2 3 5 2 6 *